HARROW TO WATFORD

Vic Mitchell and Keith Smith

 Middleton Press

Front cover: Bushey & Oxhey still had six platforms when Motor Open Brake Second no. M61140 was photographed at the front of a Broad Street train on 24th August 1957. Several main line signals are included. (A.R.Grierson/SLS)

Back cover: LMS no. 20 stands under the ornate roof at St. Albans Abbey soon after nationalisation and application of its BR number. The starting signals are also visible. (Lens of Sutton coll.)

Published August 2003
First reprint August 2008

ISBN 978 1 904474 14 2

© Middleton Press, 2003

Design   Deborah Esher
*   David Pede*
Typesetting Barbara Mitchell

Published by
*   Middleton Press*
*   Easebourne Lane*
*   Midhurst, West Sussex*
*   GU29 9AZ*
Tel: 01730 813169
Fax: 01730 812601
Email: info@middletonpress.co.uk
www.middletonpress.co.uk

Printed & bound by Biddles Ltd, Kings Lynn

CONTENTS

INDEX

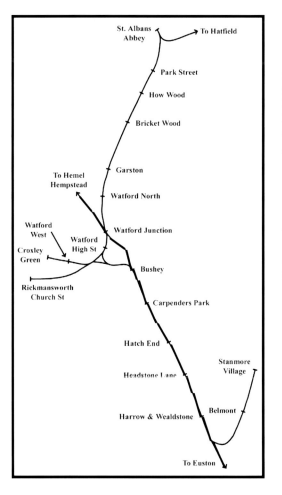

ACKNOWLEDGEMENTS

We are grateful to many of those mentioned in the credits for their assistance and also to A.E.Bennett, J.E.Connor, G.Croughton, N.Langridge, D.Lovett, Mr D. & Dr S.Salter, D.W.Smith, K.Scholey, E.Wilmshurst and finally our ever helpful wives, Barbara Mitchell and Janet Smith.

← 1.   The route diagram shows the final name used for each station. The Metropolitan Railway line to Rickmansworth of 1887 is not included and neither is its 1926 branch to Croxley Green and Watford, which is still open.

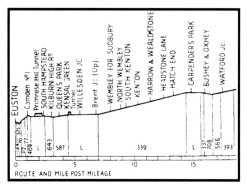

GEOGRAPHICAL SETTING

The gradient profile reveals that the route climbs almost continuously northwards, except for a dip on the approach to Watford Junction where the main line passes over the valley of the River Colne on an embankment.

Most of the route traverses London Clay, but the old established market town of Watford is on the Chalk of the dip slope of the Chiltern Hills. The town was noted for its silk mills, weaving and brewing. When built, the railway passed through a totally agricultural landscape, but the line had the unintended effect of generating an almost totally urbanised environment.

The St. Albans branch once carried pleasure seekers in large numbers to enjoy the delights of Bricket Wood, but it now has only brief rural views between the housing developments of South Hertfordshire. The city is of Roman origin and was an important place on the coach road named Watling Street.

The maps are at the scale of 25ins to 1 mile, and north is at the top, unless otherwise indicated.

HISTORICAL BACKGROUND

The route formed part of Britain's first long distance main line. The London & Birmingham Railway received its Act on 6th May 1833, but no intermediate stations were included on the section covered by this book.

Traffic began on 20th July 1837 between London and Boxmoor (Hemel Hempstead) and the LBR became part of the London & North Western Railway in 1846. Local traffic was slow to develop, but an up goods line was added between Watford and London in 1858. Single line branches were opened thus: Watford Junction to St. Albans on 5th May 1858, Watford Junction to Rickmansworth on 1st October 1862 and Harrow to Stanmore on 18th December 1890. A single line from the Rickmansworth branch to Croxley Green came into use on 15th June 1912.

The latter was part of major improvements to the entire route, which had been quadrupled in 1875 by adding a fourth track on the west side of the others. The extra two tracks would carry electric trains to Watford Junction and would diverge from the other four at Bushey to run via Watford High Street. A triangular junction was provided with the Rickmansworth branch.

The Harrow to Watford Junction section of the "New Lines" carried steam trains from 10th February 1913, electrification being delayed until 16th April 1917 due to wartime restrictions. The Bakerloo trains of the London Electric Railway then began to use the route. The power was at 630 volts DC and two conductor rails were used. LNWR electric trains reached Watford Junction on 10th January 1922 and Croxley Green on 30th October 1922. Electrification did not reach Rickmansworth until 26th September 1927. The St. Albans and Stanmore branches never received conductor rails.

The projects above were mostly undertaken by the LNWR, the main exception being that the Watford & Rickmansworth Railway Company obtained the Act for that line in 1860 and owned it until 1881, although it was always operated by the LNWR.

The London Midland & Scottish Railway took control of the lines in 1923 and they became part of the London Midland Region of British Railways upon nationalisation in 1948. Passenger services were withdrawn thus: the Rickmansworth branch on 3rd March 1952, Stanmore to Belmont on 15th September 1952 and Belmont to Harrow on 5th October 1964. The dates for freight withdrawals are given in the captions.

Electrification of the LMR main lines began in the North of England and was undertaken with overhead wires at 25,000 volts AC. Electrically hauled freight trains ran south to Willesden Junction from September 1965 and all main line services were electrically operated by 3rd January 1966. This was preceded by a short period of diesel haulage.

Local services came under the control of Network SouthEast on 18th June 1986 and most main line traffic went into the InterCity sector. AC traction was employed on the St. Albans branch from 11th July 1988. The DC services were branded the "Harlequin Line" in 1988-89 and the name "North London Railways" was applied from 31st March 1994. This also included the AC services to Birmingham via Northampton. These groups were renamed Silverlink Trains and were subject to privatisation on 2nd March 1997 when a 7½ year franchise was taken by the National Express Group. A week later, Virgin West Coast Trains took over main line operations, with the exception of ScotRail Sleeper Services, on a 15 year franchise.

PASSENGER SERVICES

Main Line

The table below indicates the number of trains calling at Harrow and Watford in sample years over the first seven decades of the line.

	Weekdays	Sundays
1837	4	4
1841	6	2
1850	10	4
1858	16	4
1869	22	5
1907	41	13

The advent of DC electrification brought a greatly increased frequency, which has been maintained from Euston at 15 to 30 minute intervals ever since.

The stopping pattern on the slow lines has varied over the years, but AC electrification brought more regular intervals and a great increase in the number of long distance trains calling at Watford Junction. An example from the steam era is shown among the timetables that follow.

Most trains have run to London, but in June 1997 Connex South Central introduced a Rugby-Gatwick Airport service. In 2003, it ran between Watford Junction (platform 10) and Brighton, usually hourly.

Bakerloo

Underground trains from Elephant & Castle ran at regular intervals daily to Watford Junction from 1917 to 1965, when the service was reduced to four trains in each of the peak periods north of Stonebridge Park. This was increased to eight in 1966, but they were withdrawn permanently in September 1982.

Harrow & Wealdstone received such trains again in the peak hours from June 1984 and all day subsequently.

St. Albans Branch

The branch was initially provided with six trains on weekdays, and two journeys on Sundays were soon added. The former figure increased to 13 by 1889 and 31 by 1911, the number remaining around 30 until February 1965 when the passing loop was removed. There were 22 trains on Sundays in the later years.

The figures were 17 and 10 until 1968, since which time they have generally been 22 and 15. There have been a few short workings, such as a 12.00 from Bricket Wood in 1966-67 and one from Watford North for factory workers in different periods.

Croxley Green Branch

The first timetable showed 18 trains, weekdays only. There were two or three trains each hour in 1935, with a regular 30 minute interval service on Sundays. A few in business hours were to and from London.

All day operation largely ceased in June 1947 and Sunday trains were withdrawn in 1959.

The 1961 timetable showed a Monday to Friday service from about 6.0 to 10.0am and from

4.0 to 8.0pm, but trains ran all day on Saturdays. There were three up and one down Broad Street services. These were withdrawn in 1968 and the branch frequencies were reduced to six in the morning and nine in the evening. However, a half-hourly interval service all day long (except Sundays) was provided from 3rd October 1988 until January 1990, when the previous figures were applied again. These were reduced to two and one in July 1991.

From May 1993 until March 1995, there was only one trip and that was before 07.00. It was subsequently provided by a bus, but the branch was still officially open.

Rickmansworth Branch

The line opened with a service of six weekday trains. This figure had doubled by 1889 and included a 5.45pm through train from Euston; there were two trips on Sundays.

Despite competition from the Metropolitan Railway from 1887, the service increased and comprised 20 weekday and 15 Sunday trains by the end of steam in 1927. Electrification brought the figures up to 31 and 28, which were maintained until 1942.

From 1943, service was suspended between about 10am and 4pm on Mondays to Fridays, but a full weekend timetable remained in force. This applied to the end in 1952.

Stanmore Branch

The first timetable showed nine trains on weekdays. A Sunday service was provided only from May 1930 to July 1947. The initial agreement with the local council banned such trains for 40 years.

By 1911, there were 35 journeys, with extras on Saturdays, trains running up to midnight. A service level of 30 to 40 each weekday was maintained until the end, although trains did not operate between about 10am and 4pm from 1950 onwards.

May 1889

LONDON, WILLESDEN, HARROW, WATFORD, ST. ALBANS, and RICKMANSWORTH.
London and North Western.

LONDON, WATFORD, CROXLEY GREEN, and RICKMANSWORTH.—London and North Western.

Miles	Down.	Week Days.																						
	Euston Station,	mrn	mrn	mrn	mrn	mrn	mrn	mrn	mrn	mrn	mrn	mrn	mrn	mrn	a	mrn	aft	aft	aft	aft	aft	aft	aft	aft
	444London....dep.	....	6 10	6 10	7 15	7 40	7 40	....	m	8 43	9 10	9 35	11 5	11 5	1140	1140	12e40	1 s 5	....	....	1s45	1 45	1e50	2s15
—	Watford.......dep.	6 30	6 50	7 20	7 55	8 13	8 25	8 46	8s58	9 40	10 5	1035	1140	1145	1230	1235	1e35	1s40	1e40	1s45	2s23	2 40	2e45	3s 2
1	Watford (High St.).	6 35	6 53	7 23	7 58	8 16	8 28	8 49	9 1	9 43	10 8	1038	1144	1148	1233	1238	1e38	1s43	1e43	1s48	2s26	2 4[illegible]	2e48	3s 5
—	Watford West	....	6 57	7 27	8 2	....	8 32	8 53	....	9 47	....	1042	....	1152	....	1242	....	....	1e47	1s52	....	2 47	....	....
—	Croxley Green ar	....	7 0	7 30	8 5	....	8 35	8 56	....	9 50	....	1045	....	1155	....	1245	....	....	1e50	1s55	....	2 50	....	....
4¼	Rickmansworth "	6 47	m	m	m	8 24	m	....	9 9	m	1016	m	1152	m	1241	m	1e46	1s51	m	m	2s34	m	2e56	3s13

Down.	Week Days—Continued.												Sundays.		
Euston Station,	aft	aft	aft	aft	aft	aft	aft	aft	aft	aft	aft	aft	aft	aft	aft	aft	aft	aft	aft	aft	aft	aft	mrn	aft	
444London........dep.	2e35	3 s 0	3 e 0	3 40	4s20	....	5 0	5 e 5	5 45	....	615	....	7 10	7s10	8 15	8 15	9 15	9s15	10s20	....	9 0	7 0	....
Watford...........dep.	3e40	3s45	3e45	4 35	4 51	5 15	5s35	5 50	6 17	6 22	6 57	7 7	7 45	7s55	8 47	8 53	9 51	10s 0	11s10	....	9 40	8 15	....
Watford (High Street)..	3e43	3s48	3e48	4 38	4 54	5 18	5s38	5 53	6 20	6 25	7 0	7 10	7 48	7s58	8 50	8 57	9 54	10s 3	11s13	....	9 43	8 18	....
Watford West........	3e47	3s52	....	4 42	....	5 22	....	5 57	....	6 29	7 4	....	7 52	....	8 54	....	9 58	....	....	....	....	....	....
Croxley Green...arr.	3e50	3s55	....	4 45	....	5 25	....	6 0	....	6 32	7 7	....	7 55	....	8 57	....	10 1	....	....	....	....	....	....
Rickmansworth ... "	m	m	3e56	m	5 5	m	5s46	m	6 28	m	m	7 18	m	8s 6	m	9 7	m	10s11	11s21	....	9 51	8 26	....

October 1912

LONDON, WILLESDEN JUNCTION, HARROW & WEALDSTONE, and WATFORD JUNCTION (Steam Services)

Miles	Down	Week Days																													
		mrn	mrn		mrn	mrn		mrn		mrn		aft		S		S	S	S		aft	S	aft	aft	S	aft	E	aft	aft	E		aft	E
	London (Euston)........dep	4 0	6 50	..	7 5	7 35	..	8 37	..	1150	..	1215	..	1230	..	1250	1 5	1 16	..	S	1 45	1 55	3 6	3 20	4 15	4 40	5 0	E	5 5	..	5 10	5 20
	" (Broad Street). "	..	..	..	..	..	..	..	..	..	..	..	..	..	..	..	..	..	..	1 15	..	..	..	..	..	..	..	4 51	..	..	..	..
5¼	Willesden Jnc. (Main Line)	4 21	..	..	7 19	7 48	..	8 51	..	12 2	..	1229	..	..	..	..	..	..	..	1 34	..	2 9	3 19	3 34	4 30	..	..	..	..	..	..	..
8¼	Wembley, for Sudbury.....	4 28	..	..	..	..	..	..	..	..	..	..	..	1245	..	..	..	1 31	..	..	..	..	..	..	..	..	..	..	..	..	..	5 35
11½	Harrow and Wealdstone...	4 35	..	..	..	7 59	..	9 3	..	..	..	..	..	1251	..	..	1 24	1 37	..	..	..	..	..	..	4 40	..	..	5 19	5 24	..	..	5 41
13¼	Hatch End, for Pinner....	..	..	..	..	..	..	..	..	..	..	..	..	1255	..	1 10	..	..	..	..	..	..	..	..	..	..	..	..	5 28	..	..	..
16¼	Bushey and Oxhey.........	..	..	..	7 32	8 6	..	..	..	..	..	..	..	1 0	..	..	..	1 44	..	1 50	..	..	..	..	..	5 3	..	5 27	5 33	..	..	5 50
17½	Watford Junction 464-7arr	4 44	7 17	..	7 37	8 11	..	9 12	..	1221	..	1246	..	1 5	..	..	1 34	1 49	..	1 55	2 12	2 26	3 37	3 51	4 49	5 8	5 27	5 32	5 38	..	5 37	5 55

Down	Week Days—Continued																		Sundays												
	aft		E		E		aft		aft		aft		aft		aft		aft			mrn	mrn	mrn	mrn		mrn	mrn		aft	aft	aft	aft	aft
London (Euston)........dep	E	..	5 42	..	5 54	..	6 6	..	E	..	6 42	..	7 15	..	9 55	..	1150	..	..	4 35	6 15	8 5	9 0	Not after 15th Sept.	1110	1135	Not after 15th Sept.	1 55	5 10	642	9 0	9 10
" (Broad Street). "	5 23	..	..	..	..	..	..	..	6 6	..	..	..	..	..	..	..	..	..	..	..	..	..	..		..	..		..	..	..	..	..
Willesden Jnc. (Main Line)	..	..	5 53	..	..	..	..	..	..	..	..	..	7 29	..	10 7	..	..	..	..	5 2	..	8 18	9 15		..	1150		2 9	..	..	..	..
Wembley, for Sudbury.....	..	..	..	..	6 9	..	..	..	..	..	..	..	..	..	..	..	..	..	..	5 7	..	..	..		..	..		..	..	..	..	..
Harrow and Wealdstone...	5 51	..	6 3	..	6 15	..	..	..	..	..	..	..	..	..	1020	..	..	..	..	5 13	..	8 28	..		..	..		..	..	..	..	9 29
Hatch End, for Pinner....	5 55	..	..	..	6 19	..	..	..	..	..	..	..	..	..	..	..	..	..	..	..	..	..	..		..	..		..	..	..	..	..
Bushey and Oxhey.........	6 0	..	..	..	6 24	..	6 31	..	6 39	..	..	..	..	..	..	..	..	..	..	..	..	8 35	..		..	..		..	..	..	..	..
Watford Junction 464-7 arr	6 5	..	6 12	..	6 31	..	6 36	..	6 44	..	7 9	..	7 47	..	1029	..	1217	..	..	5 23	6 51	8 40	9 32		1137	12 7		2 20	5 37	7 9	9 27	9 38

E or E Except Saturdays. S or S Saturdays only

August 1940

Miles		Week Days																										
		a.m	a.m	a.m	a.m		a.m	a.m	a.m		a.m	p.m	am E		am	a.m	a.m		am	am S	am S	am S		pm S	pm S	pm S	pm S	pm S
	Croxley Green ....dep	5 57	6 21	6 34	6 56	..	7 15	7 28	7 41	..	8 1	8 15	8 28	..	8 41	9 4	9 26	..	9 44	10 28	11 2	11 27	..	12 9	1234	1249	1 6	1 32
½	Watford West	5 58	6 22	6 35	6 57	..	7 17	7 30	7 42	..	8 2	8 16	8 29	..	8 42	9 5	9 27	..	9 45	10 29	11 3	11 28	..	1210	1235	1250	1 9	1 33
—	Bushey and Oxhey......	..	..	..	..	..	..	7 34	..	..	8 7	..	8 35	..	..	..	..	..	..	..	..	..	..	..	..	..	..	..
1¾	Watford (High Street)	6 2	6 27	6 39	7 1	..	7 21	..	7 46	..	..	8 20	..	..	8 46	9 9	9 31	..	9 49	10 33	11 8	11 32	..	1215	1239	1254	1 13	1 37
2¼	Watford Junction .... arr	6 5	6 29	6 42	7 4	..	7 23	..	7 49	..	..	8 22	..	..	8 48	9 11	9 34	..	9 51	10 35	11 10	11 34	..	1217	1242	1257	1 15	1 40
25	Broad Street ‡ ...... arr	7 16	..	7 47	8 8	..	..	8 33	8U38	..	9† 9	9Z13	9 26	..	9Y39	10E8	1027	..	11A10	11 46	12 24	12 34	..	1 24	1 50	2 6	2 18	2 50
20¼	London (Euston) ‡ .. "	6 47	7 22	7 42	7 55	..	8 10	8B 6	8D§27	..	8 49	9L12	9†24	..	9 38	9§52	1026	..	10§50	11 35	12 3	12 23	..	1 3	..	1 43	2 2	2§17

	Week Days—continued																												
	p.m S	pm S	pm S		pm S	p.m E		p.m S	p.m E	pm S		pm E	pm S	pm E	pm S	pm E		pm S		pm S	p.m E	pm S	pm E		pm S	pm E		pm S	pm E
Croxley Green .... dep	2 0	2 34	3 9	..	3 41	4 1	..	4 10	4 32	4 40	..	5 8	5 10	5 39	5 40	6 7	..	6 10	..	6 40	6 41	7 10	7 17	..	7 40	7 43	..	8 9	8 9
Watford West	2 1	2 35	3 10	..	3 42	4 2	..	4 11	4 33	4 41	..	5 9	5 11	5 40	5 41	6 8	..	6 11	..	6 41	6 42	7 11	7 18	..	7 41	7 44	..	8 10	8 10
Bushey and Oxhey......	..	..	..	..	..	..	..	..	..	..	..	..	..	..	..	..	..	..	..	..	..	..	..	..	..	..	..	..	..
Watford (High Street)	2 6	2 40	3 15	..	3 47	4 7	..	4 15	4 37	4 45	..	5 13	5 15	5 44	5 45	6 12	..	6 15	..	6 45	6 45	7 15	7 23	..	7 45	7 48	..	8 14	8 14
Watford Junction .... arr	2 8	2 42	3 17	..	3 49	4 9	..	4 18	4 39	4 48	..	5 15	5 18	5 46	5 48	6 14	..	6 18	..	6 48	6 48	7 18	7 26	..	7 48	7 51	..	8 17	8 16
Broad Street ‡ ...... arr	3 10	4J 3	4 43	..	5 13	5†16	..	5 43	5 38	6 14	..	6 21	6 43	6 50	7 14	7 34	..	7 43	..	8 14	7 55	8 43	8 24	..	9 14	9J 0	..	9 43	9J47
London (Euston) ‡ .. "	2 51	3 43	4 3	..	4 43	4 57	..	5 3	5†26	5 43	..	6 5	6 3	6 45	6 43	6‡53	..	6§53	..	7 43	7 34	7§54	8 14	..	8 43	8 44	..	9 8	8 59

	Sundays																												
Croxley Green ....dep	..	..	..	..	..	..	..	..	..	..	..	..	..	..	..	..	..	..	..	..	..	..	..	..	..	..	..	..	..
Watford West	..	..	..	..	..	..	..	..	..	..	..	..	..	..	..	..	..	..	..	..	..	..	..	..	..	..	..	..	..
Bushey and Oxhey......	..	..	..	..	..	..	..	..	..	..	..	..	..	..	..	..	..	..	..	..	..	..	..	..	..	..	..	..	..
Watford (High Street)	..	..	..	..	..	..	..	..	..	..	..	..	..	..	..	..	..	..	..	..	..	..	..	..	..	..	..	..	..
Watford Junction .... arr	..	..	..	..	..	..	..	..	..	..	..	..	..	..	..	..	..	..	..	..	..	..	..	..	..	..	..	..	..
Broad Street ‡ ...... arr	..	..	..	..	..	..	..	..	..	..	..	..	..	..	..	..	..	..	..	..	..	..	..	..	..	..	..	..	..
London (Euston) ‡ .. "	..	..	..	..	..	..	..	..	..	..	..	..	..	..	..	..	..	..	..	..	..	..	..	..	..	..	..	..	..

A Arr 10 55 am on Saturdays
B Change at Bushey and Oxhey. Arr 8 14 am on Saturdays
D Arr 8 34 am on Saturdays by changing at Bushey and Oxhey
E or F Except Saturdays
J Change at Willesden Junction
L Arr 9§ 2 am on Saturdays
S or S Saturdays only
U Arr 8 48 am on Saturdays
Y Arr 9 53 am on Saturdays
Z Arr 9 22 am on Saturdays
† Change at Bushey and Oxhey
‡ Via Watford (High Street)
§ Via Watford Junction
‖ Dep 6 54 am on Saturdays

February 1961

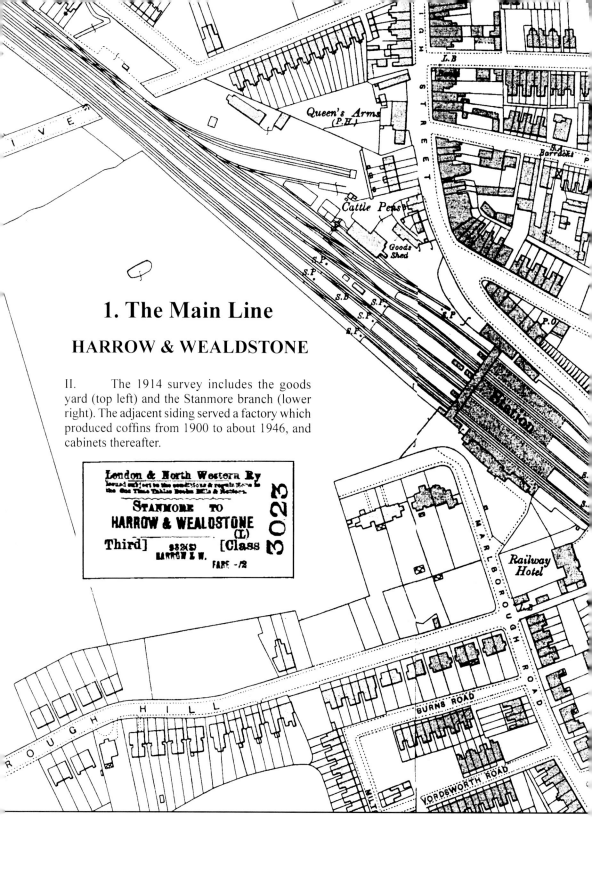

1. The Main Line

HARROW & WEALDSTONE

II.   The 1914 survey includes the goods yard (top left) and the Stanmore branch (lower right). The adjacent siding served a factory which produced coffins from 1900 to about 1946, and cabinets thereafter.

London & North Western Ry
Issued subject to the conditions & regulations in the Co's Time Tables Books Bills & Notices.

STANMORE   TO
HARROW & WEALDSTONE
(L)
Third]   932(5)   [Class
HARROW L.W.
FARE -/2

3023

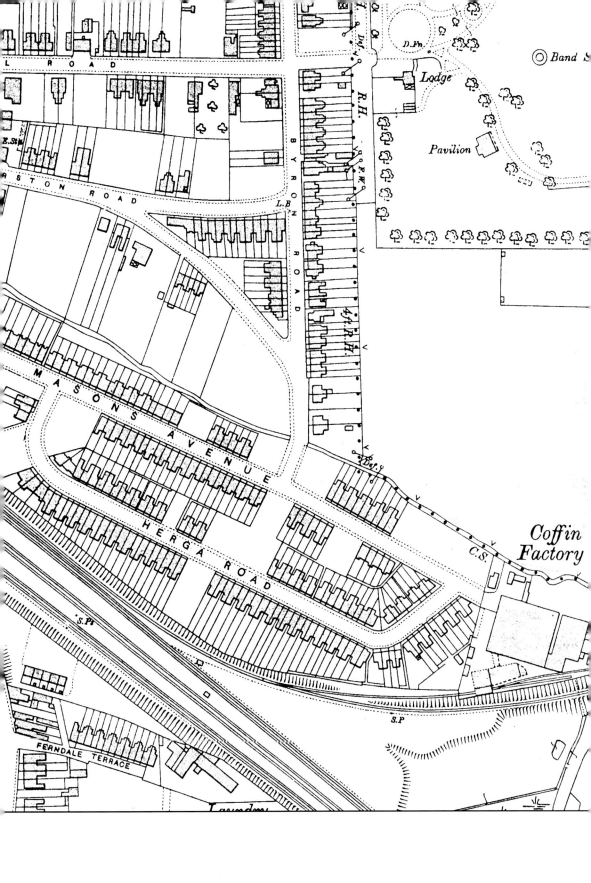

1.	A southbound train of six-wheelers enters the island platform, hauled by a "Precedent" class 2-4-0. The goods shed is behind the running-in board. The first buildings were destroyed when the up goods line was laid in 1858, when the first footbridge was built. Alterations in 1875 involved provision of two extra tracks on the west side. (Lens of Sutton coll.)

2.	The nearest of the LNWR Leyland buses is destined for Watford via Bushey Heath, while the other is on the 1½ mile long route to Harrow Town. These buildings are also on the left of the next picture and date from 1875. The suffix "and Wealdstone" was added on 1st May 1897; the LNWR bus services ceased in April 1915. (Lens of Sutton coll.)

3.	This view towards Watford is dated 1913 and shows the tracks for local trains on the left prior to the addition of conductor rails. The footbridge and the structures on the right date from the rebuilding of 1910-12, when all four through lines were moved to the right. The 1858 footbridge had been in the foreground. (LGRP/NRM)

4.	Looking towards London in the 1930s from platform 3, we see the London & Birmingham Railway's arch of the original road bridge and the steel spans of the later ones. The arch was removed in 1964. (Lens of Sutton coll.)

5.   An up electric train is in the background of this record of No. 1 Box and the goods yard. It is probably from the 1930s, when gas lighting was still in use. A vegetable oil gas plant had been built in the goods yard in 1852, but it was superseded by town gas. (Lens of Sutton coll.)

6.   On the right is the goods shed which stood from 1858 until 1969. No. 45676 *Codrington*, one of the "Jubilee" class, is standing on the goods yard points and near its ground signal. The yard closed on 3rd April 1967. (R.K.Blencowe coll.)

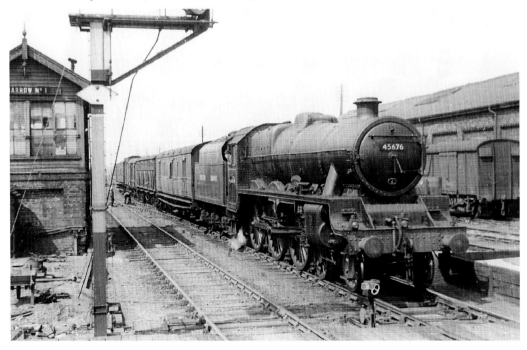

7.   Electric trains began running between Willesden Junction and here on 15th June 1912. Two coach push-pull steam trains used the new tracks northwards from 10th February 1913. A fleet of joint stock (LNWR & LER) underground trains with special raised floors and extra steps up to the platforms was introduced in 1920. Most of it was withdrawn in 1931. This ex-LNWR set is leaving on 22nd October 1952, the first day of electric operation after the dramatic collision described in the *Euston to Harrow & Wealdstone* album, hence the debris. (D.Trevor Rowe)

8.   London Transport operated Bakerloo services from 1933 and one such northbound train was recorded on 3rd October 1964, during bridge rebuilding, hence the rubbish. The Stanmore branch curves away in the centre background. This stock dates from 1938. (J.C.Gillham)

9. The track for Stanmore trains was laid on the alignment of the 1858-75 goods line in 1890 and is also seen on 3rd October 1964, which was the last day that passenger services ran on that branch. Park Royal DMU no. 50413 carries a wreath and is about to depart for Belmont; the rubble was due to the bridge works. (J.C.Gillham)

10. The second generation of electric stock was introduced in 1957 and later designated class 501. Two 3-car sets depart north on 28th February 1979, showing headcode B2, indicating a passenger train from Broad Street to Watford Junction via Primrose Hill. C was for empty stock, 1 for Euston - Watford Junction, 3 Broad Street via Kensal Rise, 4 Broad Street via Hampstead Heath, 6 to Willesden Junction, 7 to Harrow & Wealdstone, 8 to Bushey & Oxhey and 9 to Croxley Green. The 20-lever box closed on 12th December 1988 after which time the route was controlled from Willesden Junction. (T.Heavyside)

11.   The up side building was electrically lit from its completion in 1911, the generator being in a structure on its south side. There had been another wing on the left for housing bicycles until 1986. There is a chimney beside the clock tower. There is now direct access from the booking hall to platform 6. (D.Thompson)

12.   No. 321422 speeds south on 14th February 1996 and passes over the point of impact of the horrific crash of 8th October 1952. Cars are parked on the right, on the site of the goods yard, and on the left is the siding for terminating Bakerloo trains. Its points are included in picture 10. There had been two such sidings until December 1988. (M.Turvey)

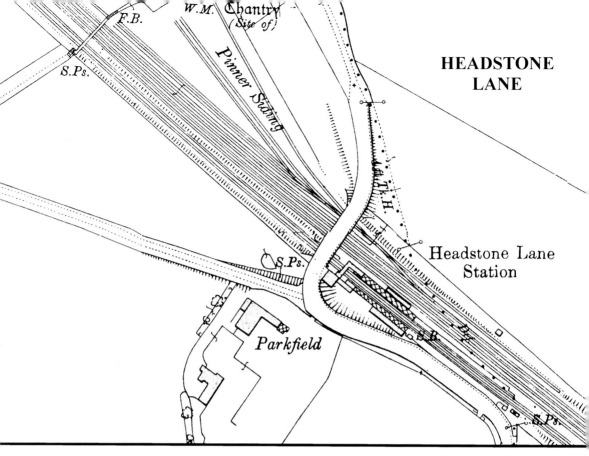

F.B.

W.M. Chantry
(Site of)

S.Ps.

Pinner Siding

T.H.

Headstone Lane
Station

S.Ps.

Parkfield

S.B.

S.Ps.

III.   The 1913 survey includes the station that was opened on 10th February of that year, but not the electricity sub-station that was built later in the goods yard, near the road bridge, and evident below.

13.   The footbridge on the left of the map was the viewpoint on 13th July 1935 for recording the 3.5pm Euston to Rugby and the goods yard, which closed on 17th November 1966. Two milk tankers are behind LNWR "Precursor" class no. 5301 *Emerald*. (K.Nunn/LCGB)

14.　　　Newspapers have been left by a northbound EMU on 3rd October 1964. BR trains did not use the centre conductor rail after 1970. This view was little changed almost 40 years later. (J.C.Gillham)

15.　　　The building is seen after the 1982 fire damage had been repaired. There had earlier been a large **UndergrounD** sign, a chimney stack and a telephone kiosk. (D.Thompson)

HATCH END

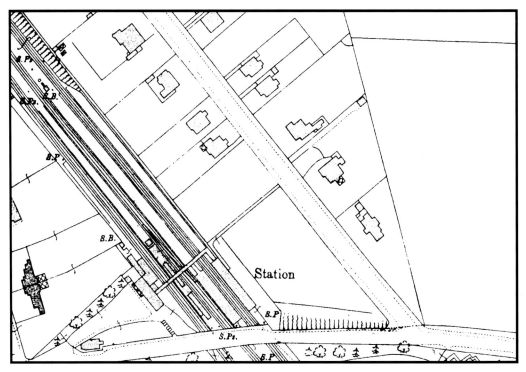

IV.   The station opened as "Pinner" on 8th April 1842, but its goods yard was nearer London and has been seen on the previous map. This is the 1913 edition.

16.   The name was set in stone during the 1911 rebuilding, although "Pinner & Hatch End" had been used since 1st January 1897. It became "Hatch End for Pinner" on 1st February 1920 and the suffix was dropped on 11th June 1956. While admiring the transport for parcels, don't miss the shelter for cabmen adorned with plant tubs. (Lens of Sutton coll.)

17.   A postcard from the 1930s shows part of the revised name and some destination options on the roof of the old post office. As at Harrow, a substantial two-tone chimney was provided. (Lens of Sutton coll.)

18.   An eastward view from the early 1950s includes an LMS "Hawkseye" nameboard and the footbridge that spanned six tracks. The platforms were numbered 1 to 6 from right to left. (Lens of Sutton coll.)

19.　　　Platforms 3 to 6 were taken out of use on 7th January 1963, having been provided with new buildings only a few years earlier. The footway from no. 6 to The Avenue was closed and the footbridge over the lines removed to receive AC wires. The remaining part is on the right of this 1964 panorama and is also in pictures 20 and 22. (J.C.Gillham)

20.　　　Two views from 1979 show a station little changed more than 20 years later. The structures on the left were replaced by a brick-built waiting shelter in 1991. (J.C.Gillham)

21.   The removal of the small canopy improved the view of the fine stone ornamentation known as "swag". The ticket office is behind the bars. This was the last station in Middlesex on the route and is now the last in the London area. (J.C.Gillham)

22.   Automatic colour light signals were installed northwards to Hatch End in June 1932. The 11.25 from Watford Junction pauses on 8th December 1993 and obscures all but the synthetic slate roof of the new waiting shelter. Note that the negative conductor rail was no longer on insulators. (M.Turvey)

"The Red Rose" Express. Patriot Class 7P locomotive. British Railways Photo.

23.   The tail of "The Red Rose" is passing through the station as "Patriot" class 4-6-0 no. 45521 *Rhyl* speeds north in the 1950s. In the background is the signal box which had 25 levers and closed on 12th July 1964. (British Railways)

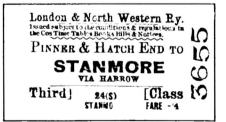

24.   Viewed from the same bridge, but in the opposite direction, are two of the original Oerlikon sets bound for Harrow on 3rd May 1957. An extra arch had been created in the bridge for the down New Line in 1911. (A.R.Grierson/SLS)

25.   Approaching Carpenders Park with a down local train on 3rd July 1946 is class 4P 2-6-4T no. 2593. This was one of a batch built by the North British Locomotive Company in 1936. On the west side of the cutting is a coal tax obelisk, which was erected under an 1861 Act and indicated the point at which a due of 1s1d per ton was levied on all coal entering London. (H.C.Casserley)

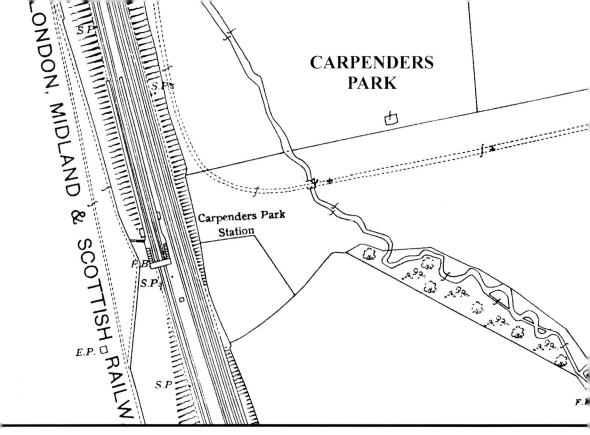

V. The 1935 edition shows the two platforms in open country, with footpath access only.

26. This view was taken from the extension of the footbridge which spanned the fast and slow lines and includes private building work in progress in about 1936. The London County Council's housing estate was started nearby in 1949 and it generated much traffic. (A.R.Grierson/SLS)

27.   The Oerlikon sets had sliding doors, one in each outer coach and two in the centre one. This feature made station stops rather prolonged. Loading is in progress on 25th August 1951. (H.C.Casserley)

28.   The two timber platforms were replaced by a single solid one, which is seen in gestation from the footbridge on 11th October 1952. (J.C.Gillham)

29.   Access to the new platform was from a tunnel which carried the footway under all the tracks. The large windows of the saloon coaches are evident as a train destined for Watford departs on 13th May 1956. (A.R.Grierson/SLS)

30.   The platform was ideally situated for afternoon train photography, such as this troop special on the down slow line on 28th July 1956. Ex-SR class N 2-6-0 no. 31413 is hauling it from Bushey to Ashford in Kent. (S.C.Nash)

31. Running on the down fast line on 29th August 1960 is no. 10202, an early example of a diesel-electric locomotive. It was built at Ashford and transferred to the LMR in 1955. (A.C.Ingram)

32. The new concrete structure can be examined as a class 501 departs for Watford on 3rd October 1964. The station was unusual in having a dimmer switch which staff could use at night to reduce the light intensity of the DC signals to avoid confusion with the signals on the AC lines. (J.C.Gillham)

33.   Viewed from the platform on 8th December 1993 is electric locomotive no. 90126 hauling a train of Ford cars. The slow lines once carried an almost continuous succession of freight trains, but space precludes inclusion of many other examples. (M.Turvey)

34.   Speeding on the up fast line on 10th June 1998 is no. 325007, which is coupled to two similar EMUs. They are bound for the Royal Mail Distribution Centre which opened at Stonebridge Park in 1996. Only first class mail is carried by rail. The demise of all UK mail trains was announced in 2003. (M.Turvey)

SOUTH OF BUSHEY

35.   Three water troughs were laid in 1864 on the level tracks in the cutting and they were the first after leaving London. "Alfred the Great" class 4-4-0 no. 1954 *Galatea* is refilling its tender while working an up express. At 40mph, about 1000 gallons could be lifted in 20 seconds. (LGRP)

36.   Overtaking an electric, this short up express is generating minimum spray. The excess water was a constant problem for the permanent way engineers, particularly in a level cutting that was difficult to drain in any case. The troughs were removed on 29th June 1965 and the reservoir site was sold to the education authority. (A.R.Grierson/SLS)

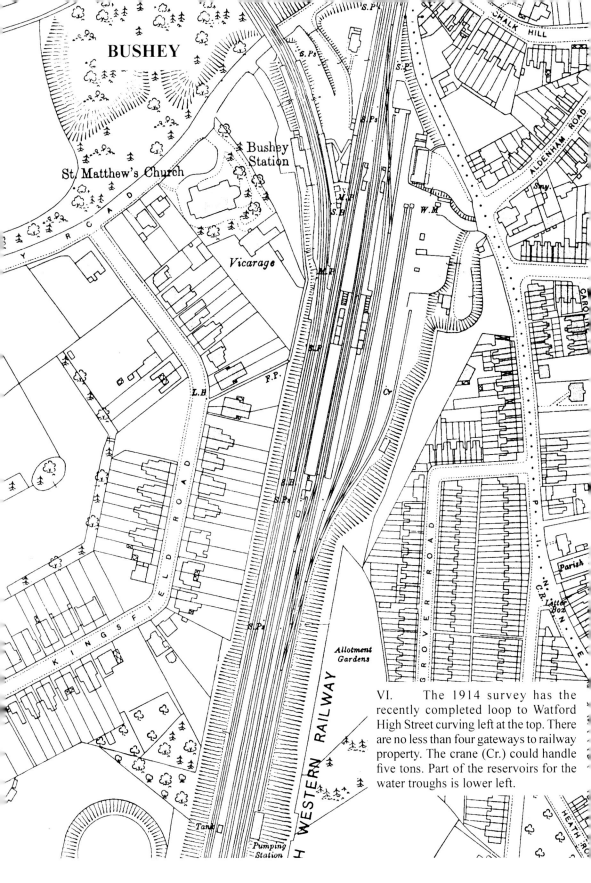

BUSHEY

St. Matthew's Church

Bushey Station

Vicarage

SHALK HILL

ALDENHAM ROAD

Smy.

W.M.

S.B.

M.P.

S.B.

S.Ps.

S.Ps.

L.B.

P.P.

Cr.

CARO

R.O.A.D.

Parish

N.C.R.

Letter Box

KINGSFIELD ROAD

GROVER ROAD

P.

S.B.

S.Ps.

S.Ps.

Allotment Gardens

HEATH RO

Tank

Pumping Station

H WESTERN RAILWAY

VI.   The 1914 survey has the recently completed loop to Watford High Street curving left at the top. There are no less than four gateways to railway property. The crane (Cr.) could handle five tons. Part of the reservoirs for the water troughs is lower left.

37.   This building was on the east side of the main lines and is seen from Pinner Road. On the left is the entrance to the goods yard, the weigh-house and the towers of three lift shafts. (Lens of Sutton coll.)

38.   This and the next picture show the platforms for quadruple track, before the addition of two curved ones for the New Lines, on the left. The goods yard was in use until 3rd February 1969, but it only handled coal after August 1968. (Lens of Sutton coll.)

← 39. The buildings were retained after the extra tracks were added and they remained standing until the 1950s. A down local train is arriving during roof repairs. The sign left of centre states WAIT HERE FOR THIRD CLASS. (Lens of Sutton coll.)

41.   Homebound daily breaders wander towards the steps, which are hidden by the lift shaft. The canopy had been removed during modernisation work. No. 75038 is accelerating the 6.12pm Euston to Bletchley on 18th May 1954. The signal box in the background had 27 levers and lasted until 12th July 1964. (H.C.Casserley)

← 40. This is a 1953 view of the building seen in picture 37. Note that a pole joins the LT and BR signs and that the weather vane is formed of a smoking tank engine. (LGRP/NRM)

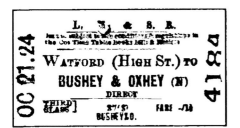

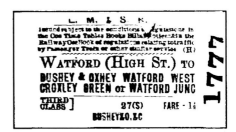

42.   Two Oerlikon sets accelerate gently (as was their custom) on 20th April 1957 and pass the down refuge siding and the pump house for the water troughs. It has a siding on the Watford side and a water tower on the other. The reservoirs are shown lower left on the map. (N.W.Sprinks)

43.   Three photographs from October 1964 complete our survey of this unusual station. Here we see the generous canopy provision on the New Line, together with the goods yard crane. (J.C.Gillham)

44.	The main line platforms had lost their luggage lifts, but retained their stairs to the subway. On the left is a modern waiting room. The down fast platform (left) was used for a display of wild shrubs in 2003. The suffix "and Oxhey" was applied from 1st December 1912 to 6th May 1974. (J.C.Gillham)

45.	A southward panorama includes an up freight train hauled by 2-8-0 no. 48122 and also the new buildings on the island platform. They were in use for a fairly short period. (J.C.Gillham)

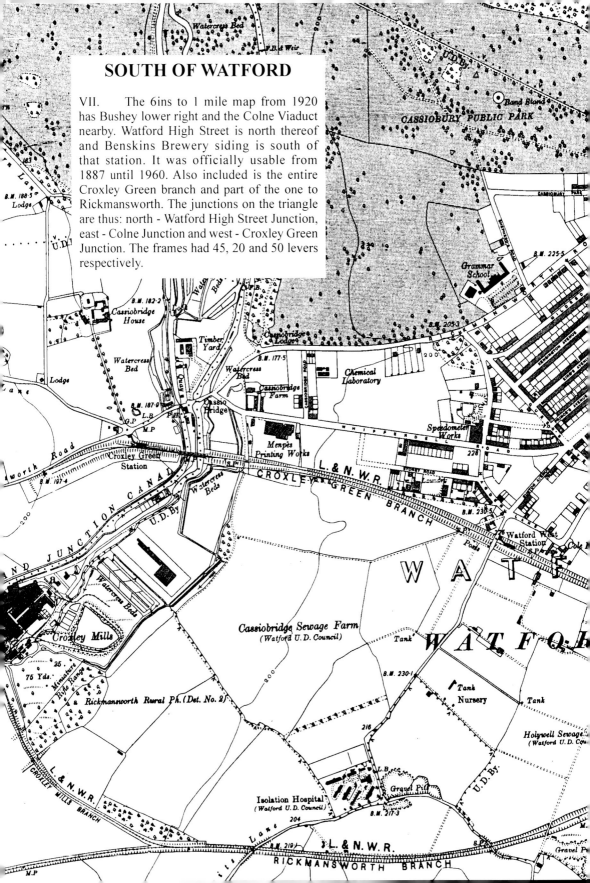

SOUTH OF WATFORD

VII.   The 6ins to 1 mile map from 1920 has Bushey lower right and the Colne Viaduct nearby. Watford High Street is north thereof and Benskins Brewery siding is south of that station. It was officially usable from 1887 until 1960. Also included is the entire Croxley Green branch and part of the one to Rickmansworth. The junctions on the triangle are thus: north - Watford High Street Junction, east - Colne Junction and west - Croxley Green Junction. The frames had 45, 20 and 50 levers respectively.

46.   High Street Junction is seen from Wiggenhall Road in 1979 as a class 501 unit proceeds towards Euston. The Rickmansworth branch had reverted to single track by that time. The signal box had been to the left of the junction and closed on 1st November 1970, along with Croxley Green Junction box. Colne Junction box had ceased to function on 18th September 1966. (J.C.Gillham)

47.   Passing the orchards north of High Street station on 13th May 1956 is one of the compartment sets based on GEC equipment and introduced in 1927. They needed shorter station stops and were used on the busier routes. Further batches arrived in 1929 and 1933. (A.R.Grierson/SLS)

WATFORD HIGH STREET

48.   The station had only a single platform from its opening in 1862 until 1912. Watford Junction was remote from the town, surrounded by fields and was the place where one changed to a train for the town centre. (British Railways)

49.   The LNWR made a good impression in the town with a vaulted roof over a carriage forecourt. The facade is little changed today, although it does have a brighter appearance. (Lens of Sutton coll.)

50.   Track doubling brought an island platform, which is seen in October 1964 with a Bakerloo train having made the penultimate stop on its northbound journey. Flower tubs enhance the dreary cutting. (J.C.Gillham)

51.   A 1992 photograph reveals the platform to be uncluttered by stanchions as the canopy is supported by trusses springing from the retaining walls. The signal in the distance has lights for a crossover used by trains to Croxley Green. (F.Hornby)

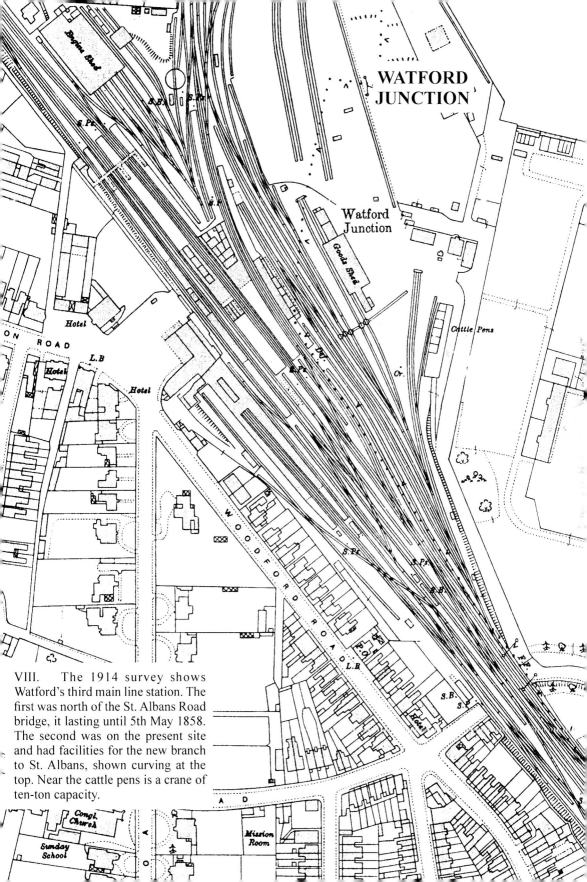

Engine Shed

S.B. S.B.

S.P.

**WATFORD
JUNCTION**

Watford
Junction

Goods Shed

Cattle Pens

Hotel

ON ROAD

L.B

Hotel

Hotel

S.P.

D.P.

Cr.

S.P.

W
O
O
D
F
O
R
D

R
O
A
D

S.P.

S.P.

S.P.

L.B

S.B.
S.P.

P.O.

F.P.

VIII. The 1914 survey shows
Watford's third main line station. The
first was north of the St. Albans Road
bridge, it lasting until 5th May 1858.
The second was on the present site
and had facilities for the new branch
to St. Albans, shown curving at the
top. Near the cattle pens is a crane of
ten-ton capacity.

A D

Congl.
Church

Sunday
School

Mission
Room

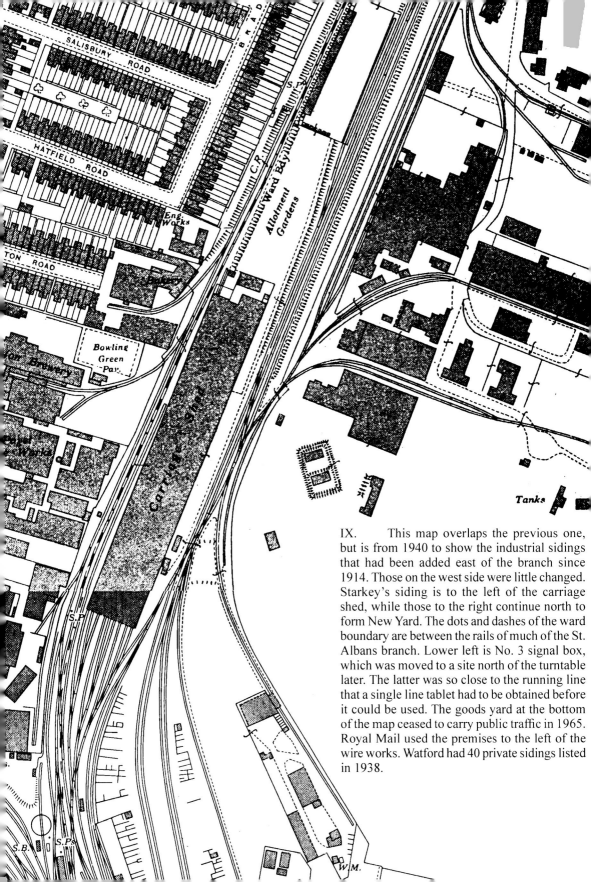

SALISBURY ROAD

HATFIELD ROAD

Eng.
Works

TON ROAD

C.P.

Allotment
Ward Bdy.
Gardens

S.P.

Bowling
Green
Pav.

on Brewery

Carriage Shed

nt Works

S.P.

S.B.

S.Ps.

Tanks

IX.   This map overlaps the previous one,
but is from 1940 to show the industrial sidings
that had been added east of the branch since
1914. Those on the west side were little changed.
Starkey's siding is to the left of the carriage
shed, while those to the right continue north to
form New Yard. The dots and dashes of the ward
boundary are between the rails of much of the St.
Albans branch. Lower left is No. 3 signal box,
which was moved to a site north of the turntable
later. The latter was so close to the running line
that a single line tablet had to be obtained before
it could be used. The goods yard at the bottom
of the map ceased to carry public traffic in 1965.
Royal Mail used the premises to the left of the
wire works. Watford had 40 private sidings listed
in 1938.

W.M.

52.   The third station was completed in 1909 and was recorded on a postcard in about 1913. The early electric light was known as a Jablachkloff Candle. (Lens of Sutton coll.)

53.   We are over the up slow line in September 1946, while 0-6-2T no. 6909 stands on the engine shed headshunt. The other locomotive is no. 6725 and it is standing at platform 11 with a train for St. Albans. Beyond it is platform 12, which is now the site of no. 11. (H.C.Casserley)

54.　　From the same viewpoint, we can imagine the sulphurous atmosphere of the shed on 14th April 1949. The works in the background produced printing ink and nearby is the air raid shelter. The shed code was 1C and it closed in March 1965. Below the water tank is the ash road and coal road. A three-road shed was recorded in 1871 and another was added in the early 1890s, but precise dates cannot be found. (H.C.Casserley)

55.　　The roofs of the building seen in picture 52 are on the left as we examine the headcode system of the Oerlikon stock. Platform 5 had a through line, but most trains terminated there as there was no connection to the main lines at its south end. (J.H.Meredith)

56.	Round head windows and doorways were everywhere in the 1909 buildings. The locomotive shed is also included in this 1953 picture. The stairway to the subway is on the right. Filming of "Brief Encounter" is recorded as having taken place at Carnforth, but much of it was shot here in 1946. These buildings were destroyed early in 1988. (LGRP/NRM)

57.	A Bakerloo train stands at platform 5, while we investigate part of the "Royal Scot" on 12th February 1954. The 10.0am from Glasgow had been derailed by a broken rail while travelling at about 65mph on 3rd February. It grazed an up Wolverhampton train; there were only 15 minor injuries. (R.M.Casserley)

58.   The St.Albans train is departing in the Summer of 1955 behind 2-6-2T no. 40043 and is about to pass between MacMillans Iron Foundry and the carriage sheds. On the left is No. 3 Box; it ceased to function on 23rd November 1973. (A.W.V.Mace/Milepost 92½)

59.   The RCTS operated a railtour which ran via Hatfield to St. Albans Abbey from where the seven coaches were hauled by class 7F 0-8-0 no. 49431 (left) into platform 12. The other branches included in this album were also visited in short trains; 0-4-4T no. 41909 is returning with one such trip on 30th April 1955. (R.S.Carpenter)

60.   "Patriot" class 4-6-0 no. 45547 passes through platform 9 with an up freight on 25th July 1957 and we obtain a glimpse of the station masters house above the second van. (B.W.Leslie)

61.   This panorama is from platforms 3 and 4 in October 1964. The track was later removed from no. 5. No. 4 Box is featured; it controlled the DC tracks only and closed on 8th January 1967. (J.C.Gillham)

62.   A DMU departs for St.Albans as loco coal wagons stand adjacent to the turntable road. The close proximity of the turntable pit to the line from platform 10 is evident. (R.Taylor)

63.   The south of the station was recorded on 28th February 1979 as a class 310 unit departs on the up slow line. This type was displaced by 317s in November 1998. Several class 313s are berthed in sidings on the left and they have to reach them from the DC lines (right) by elevating their pantographs and traversing all the crossovers seen in this view. (T.Heavyside)

64.	A panorama from November 1981 has the DC terminal platforms on the right, together with the former fish dock. The buffet is to the left of the poster board and the parcel office is to the left of that. (P.Drummond)

65.	The booking hall lantern roof was to the left of the clock tower seen in the centre of the previous picture. This record is also from 1981. (P.Drummond)

66.   Work started on the new station block in April 1984 and its official opening took place on 26th September 1985. The cost was £15m, but this did not include replacement of the buildings seen in picture 56. (D.Thompson)

67.   Two 3-car class 501 units leave from platform 4 on 11th May 1985 and pass the signal box which came into use on 12th July 1964 to control the main lines between North Wembley and Cheddington. No. 1 Box (112 levers) and No. 2 Box (54 levers) closed that day. Red panels on the blinds were provided on this stock on the Southern Region, but not here. (J.C.Gillham)

68.   Intended to entice M25 users from their cars, the station was rebuilt in the most inhospitable style possible, with no weather protection whatsoever. These are the fast line platforms where trains to all cities to Inverness call with commendable frequency. The platform buildings were completed in September 1989. (D.Thompson)

69.   Recorded on 8th December 1993 were platforms 2 to 4, onto which DC line passengers have been ejected into the rain. They also have to suffer overcrowding, as class 313s can only operate as single units due to current supply limitations, although the voltage has been increased to 700. (M.Turvey)

2. St. Albans Branch

X.   St. Albans is top right on this 1945 map at 1ins to 1 mile and below it is Park Street, the first stop down the branch. Below this is an embankment which carried a connection to the Midland Railway, near Napsbury, during the construction of this line in 1868. The A500 formed the Watford bypass and a goods depot was created beside it. It is shown in detail on map XIV.

XI.   The 1925 edition at 6ins to 1 mile shows Callowland Halt, which opened on 1st October 1910 and became Watford North on 1st March 1927. It would soon become surrounded by industry and housing.

70.   A northward view in 1946 features the extensive shelter provided for factory workers and a curiously shaped dwelling for the crossing keeper. Also evident is the small signal box, which housed a six-lever ground frame. Staffing ceased on 16th January 1966. (H.C.Casserley)

71.   This 1998 photograph includes the mirror for driver-only operation (anticipated but not practised), an extension to the curious cottage, equipment for driver activation of the barriers on Bushey Mill Lane (installed on 11th December 1966) and a signal for the remaining siding, albeit long closed. (F.Hornby)

Watford North Station

L.B.

Infants School

PARKGATE ROAD

SOUTHWOLD ROAD

Tank

Tank

...NDRINGHAM ROAD

BM 248·65

SANDOWN ROAD

WINDSOR ROAD

Chy

L.M.S.R.

ST.ALBANS BRANCH

OSBORNE ROAD

BM 247·00

SOUTHFIELD AVEN...

BALMORAL ROAD

XII.   This 1940 map is a continuation of no. IX and reveals that the cocoa factory shown on no. XI had been adapted for other purposes. The platform shelter is shown top right. Balmoral Road passes under the line and a freight concentration depot of this name was opened on 31st December 1962 to serve the surrounding district.

T.C.B.

...TH ROAD

...HAW ROAD

...E GROVE

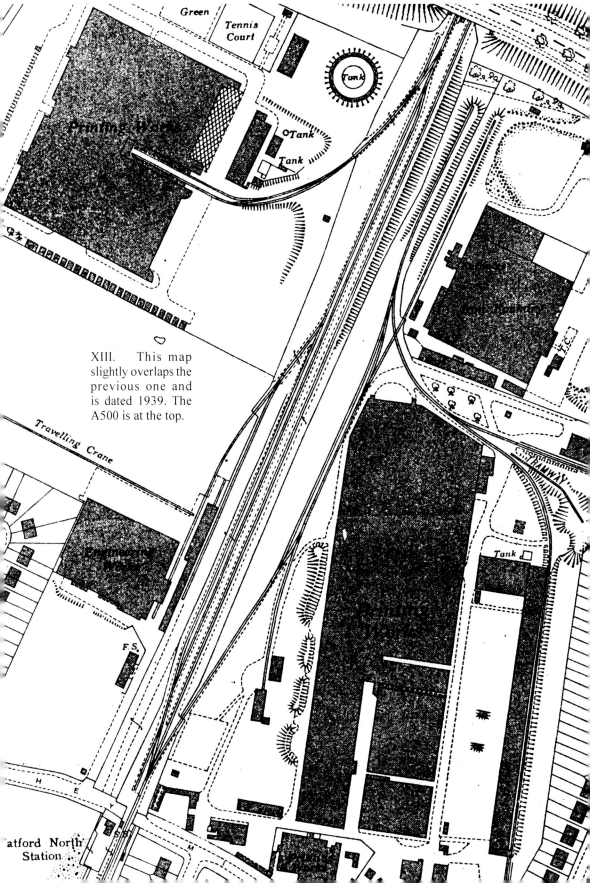

Green

Tennis
Court

Tank

Printing Works

Tank

Tank

XIII. This map
slightly overlaps the
previous one and
is dated 1939. The
A500 is at the top.

Travelling Crane

TRAMWAY

Tank

F.S.

H
E
Y

atford North
Station

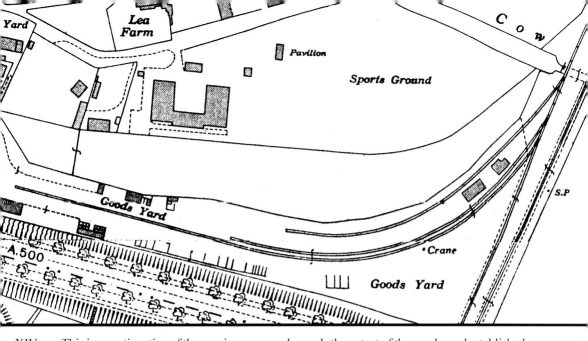

XIV.   This is a continuation of the previous map and reveals the extent of the goods yard established on 1st October 1910 by the LNWR to serve local industry. General traffic ceased on 1st April 1970, but heating oil continued. Loads of Pedigree Dog Food began to arrive on 21st September 1987. Stone for the M25 also arrived here, but the yard closed in 1988. The crane would lift ten tons.

GARSTON

72.   The platform is on the east side of the line and came into use on 7th February 1966 to serve an extensive residential development. The white cross on a blue board indicates to drivers that the audible warning received in the cab is applicable only when running in the other direction. The line passes under the M1 half a mile beyond the station. (P.Drummond)

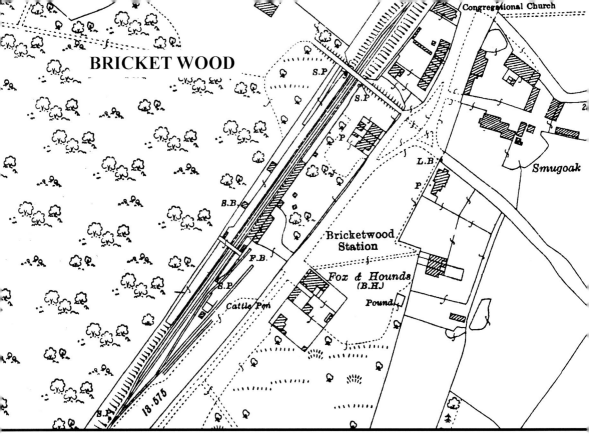

BRICKET WOOD

Congregational Church

S.P

S.P

Smugoak

P

L.B

P

B.B

Bricketwood
Station

Fox & Hounds
(B.H.)

F.B.

S.P

Pound

Cattle Pen

18.675

XV.   From its earliest days, the station was the destination of Londoners seeking a day in the surrounding woodland. This 1924 edition reveals its proximity. However, the stop was closed from 1st August 1858 for about three years. There were no staff and probably no buildings in the early years.

73.   A wooden building on the east side served until the 1890s, when it was replaced by a brick structure. There is a rustic footbridge in the background. Initially the spelling was Brickett Wood. (Lens of Sutton coll.)

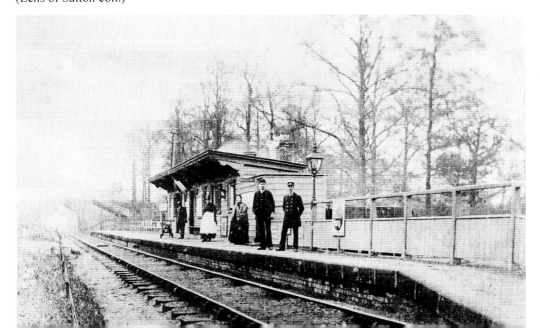

74.   A substantial canopy was provided in the days when passenger welfare was considered important, but the photographer was more interested in recording the holiday crowds than the complete locomotive. Nearby was Gray's Funfair, which included one of Britain's first 10¼ ins gauge railways. Joyland was added, but both declined and closed in 1929. (Lens of Sutton coll.)

75.   The crowds increased so much in the new century that an additional platform was provided in August 1913, on the down side, along with a signal box. This could be switched out at quiet times or when only one platform was required. (Lens of Sutton coll.)

76.　　The 1.50pm from Watford Junction was worked by no. 41220 on 25th June 1955. The new platform would take ten coaches. The date of the first siding cannot be found but the second was added in 1888. The goods yard was later occupied by a builders merchant. (D.Trevor Rowe)

77.　　Trains passed here regularly for many years and there are starting signals at the St. Albans end of both platforms. The footbridge was dismantled and rebuilt at Caledonian Road & Barnsbury on the North London Line. The signal box had an 18-lever frame and closed on 7th August 1966, when the loop was taken out of use. (N.W.Sprinks)

78.   Class 313s have monopolised the services since electrification in 1988, but they require a crew of three. This is partly due to lack of track circuits north of Garston. This February 2002 photo includes part of the brick building which had been totally sealed up long ago. (F.Hornby)

NORTH OF BRICKET WOOD

79.   During the construction of the M25 in the mid-1980s, it was necessary to divert the branch by inserting four small-radius curves, with check rails. The normal alignment is on the left; the area was excavated and a long bridge was built in the hole. (P.Drummond)

HOW WOOD

80.　　　Further residential development justified yet another station. This opened on 22nd October 1988 and was built on the east side. The entrance is near the shelter. (D.Thompson)

PARK STREET

XVI.　　　The first station opened with the line and was situated near the later junction with the temporary line to the MR described in caption X. It was unstaffed in its first years and was moved northwards half a mile to a site close to Watling Street (A5 from 1919) on 24th May 1890. The suffix "& Frogmore" was applied from that time until 6th May 1974. The River Ver is close to the line here and is marked with a flow direction arrow on this 1924 map. The single siding was used mostly for the receipt of coal and closed on 3rd May 1965.

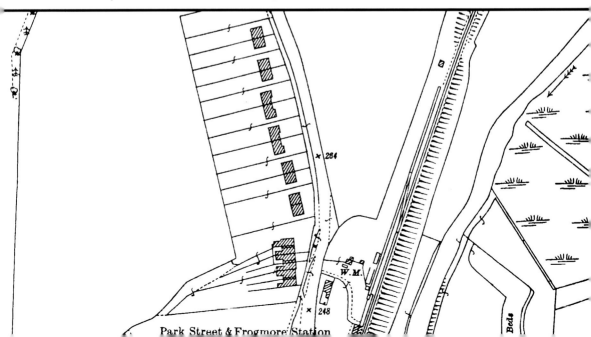

Park Street & Frogmore Station

81.   The station building was timber framed and clad, as was the platform. The signal was controlled from Hyde Lane crossing where the gates were normally kept closed across the road. The sole remaining employee was withdrawn in 1966. (Lens of Sutton)

82.   All traces of the historic structures were removed and were replaced by the standard components used elsewhere on the branch. (D.Thompson)

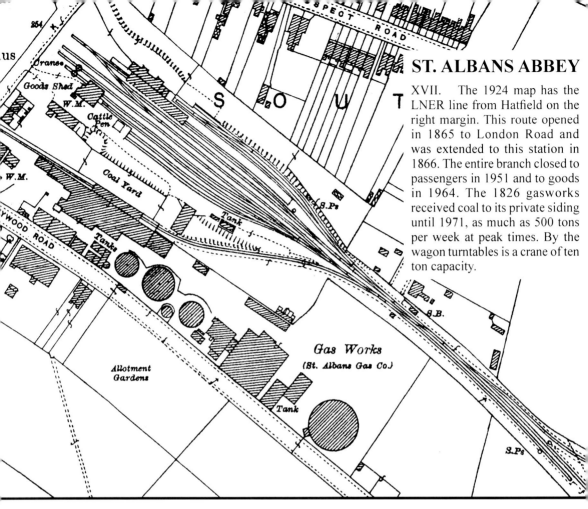

ST. ALBANS ABBEY

XVII.   The 1924 map has the LNER line from Hatfield on the right margin. This route opened in 1865 to London Road and was extended to this station in 1866. The entire branch closed to passengers in 1951 and to goods in 1964. The 1826 gasworks received coal to its private siding until 1971, as much as 500 tons per week at peak times. By the wagon turntables is a crane of ten ton capacity.

83.   A 1930 panorama features the elegant train shed which had eight spans; these were reduced to five in about 1947. All the glass had been removed during the war. On the right is a horse box, a reminder that the Royal Army Veterinary Corps had its equine hospital nearby. (LGRP/NRM)

84.   The 6.0pm from Watford Junction arrives on 11th August 1945 behind 2-6-2T no. 43. The lines on the left were used by LNER trains and those on the right were for goods traffic. This ceased on 5th October 1964 and the yard is now occupied by Sainsbury's car park. The 25-lever signal box closed on 7th August 1966. (H.C.Casserley)

85.   The bay platform was added in about 1900 and standing at it in August 1945 was LNER class N1 0-6-2T no. 4577 with the 7.0pm departure for Hatfield. There were only two trains a day in the final years of this route. (H.C.Casserley)

86.　　　The station was known as "St. Albans LNWR" until it became "St. Albans Abbey" on 2nd June 1924. The north elevation is seen in 1953. Staffing ceased on 16th January 1966 and demolition followed. (LGRP/NRM)

➜　87. Corrugated iron over the platform was considered to be the ideal treatment for the glassless roof, but subsequent managers felt that destruction was the best option. An English Electric diesel "rail coach" was tried in 1934 and AC cars were trialled in 1952. This is one of two 3-car sets from British United Traction introduced on 25th July 1955. Of limited success, they shared duties with steam until conventional DMUs were introduced. These ran on the branch for about 20 years. (M.J.Stretton coll.)

➜　88. Occasionally class 321s appear on the route, this example being recorded on 8th February 1992. The platform had been greatly shortened at the far end. (F.Hornby)

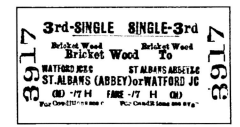

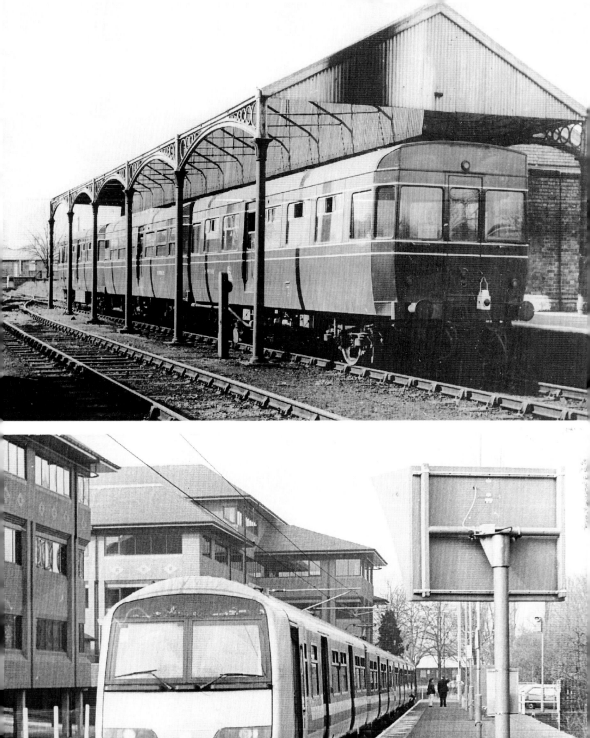

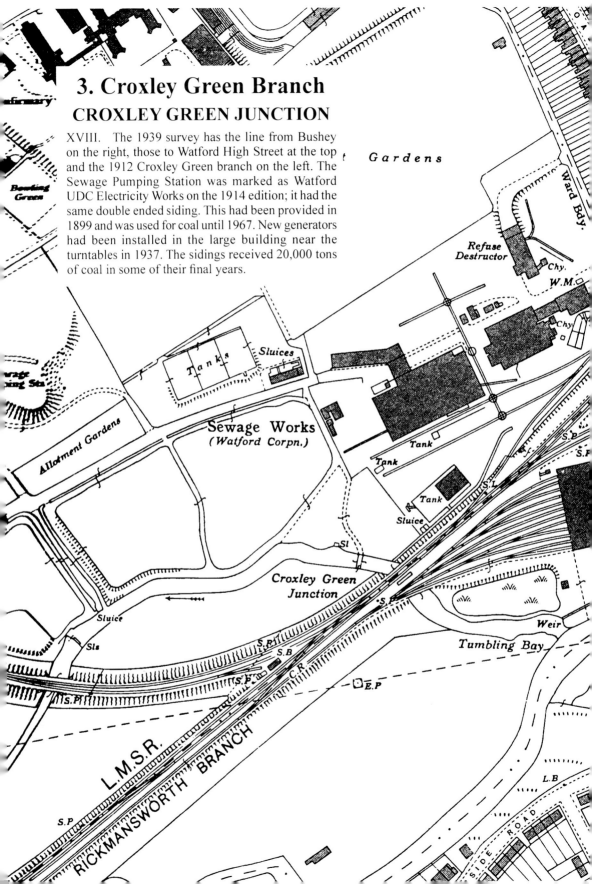

3. Croxley Green Branch
CROXLEY GREEN JUNCTION

XVIII.   The 1939 survey has the line from Bushey on the right, those to Watford High Street at the top and the 1912 Croxley Green branch on the left. The Sewage Pumping Station was marked as Watford UDC Electricity Works on the 1914 edition; it had the same double ended siding. This had been provided in 1899 and was used for coal until 1967. New generators had been installed in the large building near the turntables in 1937. The sidings received 20,000 tons of coal in some of their final years.

Gardens

Ward Bdy.

Refuse Destructor

Chy.

W.M.

Chy.

Bowling Green

Sluices

Tanks

Sewage Works
(Watford Corpn.)

Tank

Tank

Tank

Sluice

Allotment Gardens

S.B

S.P

Sl

Croxley Green
Junction

S.P

Sluice

Sls

Weir

Tumbling Bay

S.B

S.P

C.R

E.P

L.M.S.R.

RICKMANSWORTH BRANCH

L.B

S.P

SIDE ROAD

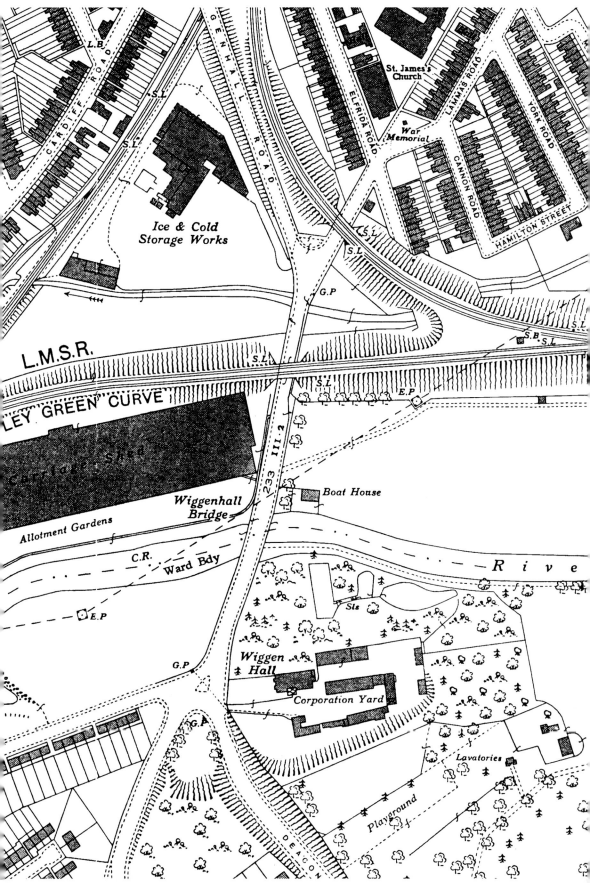

89.   Two photographs from October 1978 show parts of the twelve-road shed which was exclusively electric and so confirmed by the notice STEAM ENGINES MUST NOT ENTER THIS SHED. The lines therein were first energised on 16th April 1917 and each one accommodated 12 cars. (B.Morrison)

90.   This was a unique location for a line-up of class 501s. Within the shed, power could be obtained from trolleys on the overhead rails, by plugging the vertical cables into the end of the trains. The depot closure was 2nd November 1985. (B.Morrison)

91.   The last train to leave the shed was hauled by a diesel on 2nd December 1987. In the background is the second power station on that site; it was provided with a siding for gas oil in 1977, but only a few trains used it, for political reasons. The overhead DC system is seen again. In the future, all the local stock would be maintained at Hornsey Depot and stabled at stations overnight. (P.Drummond)

WATFORD STADIUM

92.   The platform was on the south side of the line and was opened by Elton John, chairman of Watford Football Club, on 4th December 1983. It was able to accept six-car trains and was intended for use by visiting fans, but very few trains ever called here. It was still shown on the national rail map 20 years later! (D.Thompson)

WATFORD WEST

93.　　The location is shown on map VII (after picture 45) and the exterior was probably photographed in the 1960s. It is likely to be the middle part of the day, as the doors are closed. A double shift system was worked until the clerk was withdrawn in 1989. (Lens of Sutton coll.)

→　94. One of the GEC compartment sets stands at the platform which would appear to accommodate six coaches. Such units worked to Broad Street in the peak hours in tandem. (N.F.Gurley)

→　95. The station was named Hagden Lane initially and was closed during part of World War I. The bridges were built for double track, but it never materialised. This view is from the NSE era when the branch was in terminal decline. (D.Thompson)

L.M.&S.R.FOR CONDITIONS SEE BACK
EXCESS FARE EXCHANGE TICKET
WATFORD WEST TO
LONDON(EUSTON)orOXFORD CIRCUS
VIA QUEENS PARK
Valid only on date shewn hereon after 4 0.p.m.
Not valid for break of journey. Issued in exchange
for GREEN LINE COACH RETURN
TICKET No.
THIRD CLASS 　　　1380(S[H]I) EXCESS CHARGE
EUSTON LC　　　.........D

CROXLEY GREEN

96.   The simple layout of a loop with two sidings beyond is shown on map VII. The bridge on the left passes over the Grand Junction Canal and the River Gade. Also featured is the LNWR's "Collection Van". (Lens of Sutton coll.)

97.   No details survive of this staff photograph unfortunately. Identifiable is the station master (centre) and a guard on the left. The hut appears in picture 99. (Lens of Sutton coll.)

98.	The scene on 1st March 1952 includes one of the 1916 Oerlikon sets exposing one lamp; coal wagons are in the yard, which closed on 14th November 1966. Sugg's Rochester pattern gas lights add a little elegance to a drab view. (J.C.Gillham)

99.	Another 1952 record and this includes the limit of the 1922 conductor rails and the end of the run-round loop, used until that time by passenger train locomotives. The LMS sign was still in place. (H.C.Casserley)

100.   The top of the staircase, BR totem signs and Watford power station's chimneys are evident in this record from the late 1950s. Fire buckets are lined up; there had been an arson attack soon after the opening. (Lens of Sutton coll.)

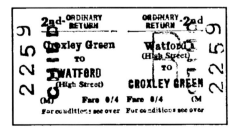

101. The inclination of the trees confirm that this was a windswept location. It is seen in November 1979 after the original booking office had been demolished. The platform and remaining building became unsafe in 1989 and both were also removed. (J.C.Gillham)

102. A temporary platform was erected opposite the original one in 1989 and staffing ceased. A full weekday service was provided from June until the following January, but as there was seldom a conductor to collect fares, the statistics justified withdrawal of the service. However, the line was legally open when photographed in May 2003, although a large section of embankment had been removed for road improvements - modern railway politics at their best! (P.Drummond)

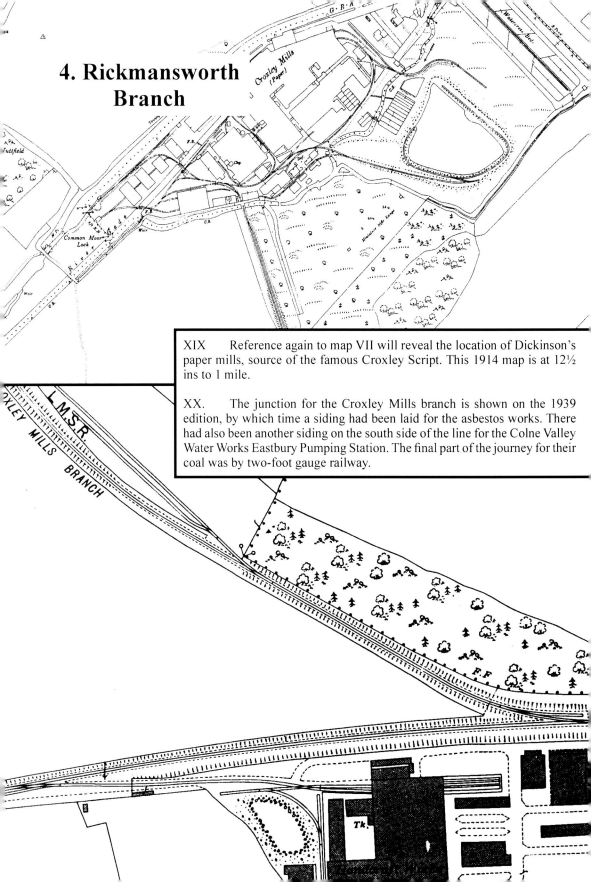

4. Rickmansworth Branch

XIX   Reference again to map VII will reveal the location of Dickinson's paper mills, source of the famous Croxley Script. This 1914 map is at 12½ ins to 1 mile.

XX.   The junction for the Croxley Mills branch is shown on the 1939 edition, by which time a siding had been laid for the asbestos works. There had also been another siding on the south side of the line for the Colne Valley Water Works Eastbury Pumping Station. The final part of the journey for their coal was by two-foot gauge railway.

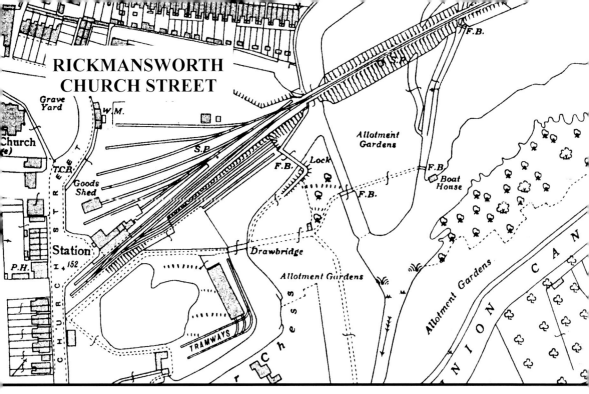

XXI. The terminus was centrally situated and closely associated with water transport. Locks are shown on both the Grand Union Canal and the River Chess, the latter being navigable to Salter's Brewery. This is the 1935 survey; the 1932 edition did not show the tramways and associated two private sidings of a timber merchant. The 1871 canal basin north of the drawbridge had a travelling crane for railway/canal transfer.

103. Sugg's Windsor pattern of gas lamp adorned this outpost of the former LNWR seen in 1951, by which time BR totem signs were attached to their posts. A true branch, we have found no evidence of direct through working to London. The flat-roofed hut housed the lever frame. (H.C.Casserley)

104. The original timber built structure of 1862 was replaced by this building in 1921-22, in good time to receive electric trains in 1927. Staff transport and a train were recorded in 1951. To make a distinction from the Metropolitan Line station, "Church Street" was added on 25th September 1950. (H.C.Casserley)

105. Timber stacks and the lines to the canal wharf are included in this view of an Oerlikon set waiting to depart on 2nd March 1952. The station masters office was on the extreme right of the building. (J.H.Meredith)

106.   GEC stock stands with a tail lamp in place on 20th February 1952. Only the coach with the louvered electrical compartment had motors. There had earlier been a substantial watercress traffic from this station. (D.B.Clayton)

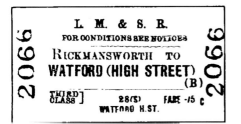

L. M. & S. R.
FOR CONDITIONS SEE NOTICES
RICKMANSWORTH   TO
WATFORD (HIGH STREET)
                                (B)
THIRD
CLASS]   28(S)   FARE -/5 C
          WATFORD H.ST.
2066   2066

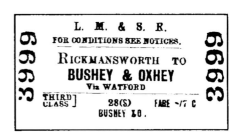

L. M. & S. R.
FOR CONDITIONS SEE NOTICES.
RICKMANSWORTH   TO
BUSHEY & OXHEY
Via WATFORD
THIRD
CLASS]   28(S)   FARE -/7 C
          BUSHEY 10.
3999   3999

107.   Three signals and the spacious saloon of an Oerlikon driving trailer are included in this view from 1st March 1952, two days before official cessation of passenger service. (J.C.Gillham)

→ 108.   No. 41909 and its two coaches have already been seen in picture 59. The date is 30th April 1955 and the goods yard was still busy; it remained in use until 2nd January 1967. (S.C.Nash)

→ 109.   No. 41901 hauled a LCGB railtour on 28th June 1958. The trip from St. Pancras to Euston included Newport Pagnell and Wolverton. On leaving this station, the running number was displayed as M969. The western part of the branch is now a cycle track. (D.Lawrence)

5. Stanmore Branch

BELMONT

XXII.   Although the branch opened in 1890, a stop was not provided here until 12th September 1932. The 1936 survey indicates extensive development of semi-detached housing, but that the Belmont Circle shopping centre was not yet complete.

➔ 110.   As the map shows, there was initially only one platform face in use. A temporary siding for the delivery of bricks is recorded - it may have been here. The driver of 2-6-2T no. 20 is receiv-ing the right-away from the porter, as steam trains did not carry guards on this branch. (Lens of Sutton coll.)

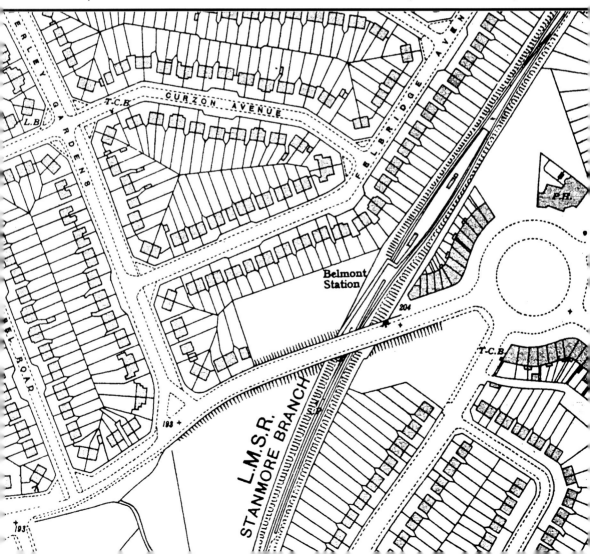

111.   A full canopy, permanent buildings and a passing loop were in use from 5th July 1937 and are seen in April 1952, along with an LMS Hawkseye sign. (H.C.Casserley)

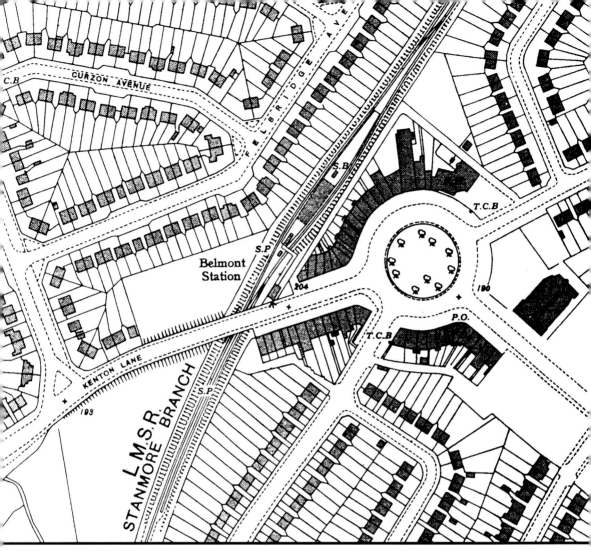

XXIII. The 1939 edition includes the new premises and footbridge. The sidings were for safety purposes and ended in sand-drags.

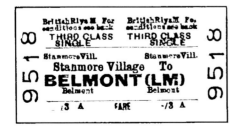

112.　　Propelling its train to Stanmore on 12th April 1952 is 2-6-2T no. 40043. All trains called at this platform when the loop was not in use and a long staff was employed on the branch. It could be used to unlock the frame here and electric tablets could then be released for each half of the line. (H.C.Casserley)

113.　　The station became the branch terminus for passengers on 15th September 1952. First generation BUT railcars were in use in most of the 1954-61 period, but steam traction then returned intermittently until 15th December 1962. Two Park Royal vehicles were recorded waiting to reverse under the footbridge on 17th September 1962. (T.Wright)

114.   A small crowd appeared on the last day of operation, 3rd October 1964; the train also appears in picture no. 9. The posters were offering trips to Kew Gardens for 3/8 or Richmond for 3/9. (J.C.Gillham)

115.   Seen on the same day is the end of one of BRs shortest branches. The loop had been removed in November 1957, but the track beyond the stops continued in use until July 1964. (J.C.Gillham)

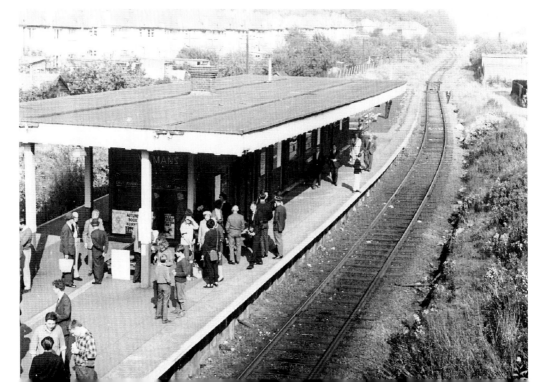

STANMORE VILLAGE

XXIV. The 1914 survey recorded a few spacious mansions, areas of woodland and a boat house on the lake. Many folk had resisted the proposal for a railway in this peaceful rural area, which had a population of under 1500.

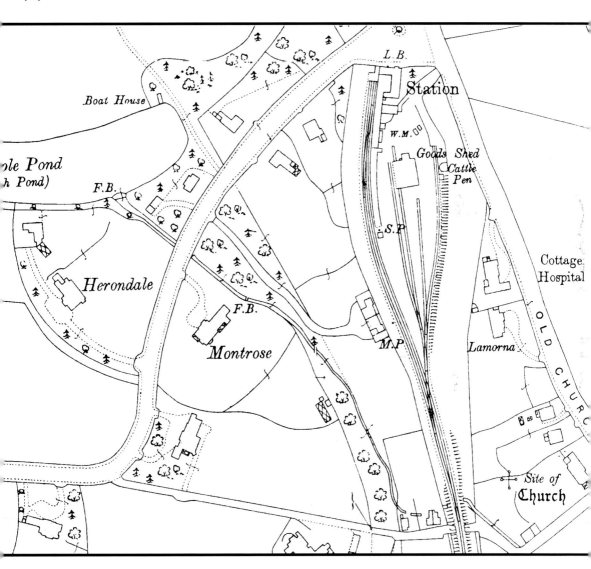

116.   A Gothic ecclesiastical style was agreed to appease the local council, but the buttressed portico, the stone clock case and the four large gargoyles were all removed in the mid-1950s. In 1970, Harrow Council failed to appreciate the merits of the building and allowed the mutilation of its remaining features, the spire and tower both being removed! (Lens of Sutton coll.)

117.   Massive floral baskets hang under the elaborately ornamented awning. Its glass was replaced by corrugated asbestos after World War II and two stanchions and associated roofing were removed in about 1950. (LGRP/NRM)

118.   No. 6408 was one of ten class 2P 0-4-4Ts introduced by Stanier in 1932. It was in that year that the Metropolitan Railway's Bakerloo Line reached Stanmore and abstracted most of the traffic from the LMS branch. The word "Village" was added to the name on 25th September 1950. (M.J.Stretton coll.)

➔   119.   We end our visit to this once-elegant outpost of the LNWR with a panorama from September 1950, when the line was still busy at peak times, but the coaches were left in the loop during the day. Passenger service was withdrawn on 15th September 1952, but goods traffic lasted until 6th July 1964, coal and bananas being the main traffic. Electrification materials were stored here and the last train left with these on 21st August 1964, the station never benefitting from such modernisation. (R.S.Carpenter)

➔   120.   There was a Civil Defence use in 1958-59 when the sign stated 19th MIDDLESEX HOME GUARD BATTALION. The fine details and the carefully carved battlements survived Hitler's activities, but not those of subsequent local councillors. (P.C.Wheeler)

Middleton Press

EVOLVING THE ULTIMATE RAIL ENCYCLOPEDIA

Easebourne Lane, Midhurst, West Sussex.
GU29 9AZ   Tel:01730 813169

www.middletonpress.co.uk   email:info@middletonpress.co.uk
A-978 0 906520 B- 978 1 873793 C- 978 1 901706 D-978 1 904474 E - 978 1 906008

OOP Out of print at time of printing - Please check availability   BROCHURE AVAILABLE SHOWING NEW TITLES